INCARNATION
OF
GOD

Written by Best Selling Author:

Maria Iskander

INCARNATION OF GOD

Copyright © Maria Iskander, 2022

ISBN: 978-0-6454631-5-6 Hardcover

ISBN: 978-0-6454631-6-3 Ebook

First published 2022

ACKNOWLEDGEMENTS

I acknowledge and value the cultural histories, heritage, and traditions of Aboriginal and Torres Strait Islander people. It is my hope that you will join my vision to educate ourselves, our families, and our greater community about unity, understanding, acceptance and meaningful connections.

Finally, I want to thank the Jagera Peoples: the Traditional Custodians of the Land on which I wrote this book.

INCARNATION OF GOD — Maria Iskander

CONTENTS

Chapter Five

The Victorious Resurrection 29

Chapter Six

Rejected By His Own 35

Chapter Seven

The Power of Love 41

Chapter One

Recognising God

'You have been set free from sin and have become slaves to righteousness.'

I am using an example from everyday life because of your human limitations. "Just as you used to offer yourselves as slaves to impurity and to ever-increasing wickedness, so now offer yourselves as slaves to righteousness leading to holiness" (Romans 6:18-19).

To take a step further in our rich Orthodox faith, one must also consider the relevance of God, the Word and His manifestation into Man. God's Divine Apparition in our midst was for the salvation of all mankind. God the Word and Creator, being without beginning or end, is the same God who came to our Earth for our salvation. Contrary to the faith, many Epicureans in this day and age for instance, believe that the Earth formed on its own—without a Creator. This ignorant claim by the Epicureans denies the existence of not only God but also themselves. Ironically, at times when we ignorantly sin, we follow the Epicureans and deny God the Maker and Artificer of all creation. Our sins have the same dire consequence as our forefather Adam and foremother Eve. When our God secured grace in the law and place of Paradise He instructed, "The knowledge of good and evil ye shall not eat, but in the day that ye do eat, ye shall surely die." When this condition was broken Adam and Eve were prohibited from living in Paradise. Likewise, our sins prohibit our path to even attain Paradise. Our God already came down on Earth and was crucified for our sorry case of transgression. So whenever we transgress, may we be haste to repent. A true repentance ensures that the envy of the devil becomes diminished. What is more, our true repentance creates our God's sacrifice on the cross to be no longer in vain and you and I, once again, become incorruptible children of God (not the devil). What a concept!

Your Love Embraced Me

As a teen, our emotions and expectations versus reality go into havoc. So in the context of sin, it can be easy to wrongly think that God will reach a point when He will not accept us. Perhaps we struggle with praying or reading the Holy Bible. Or maybe we struggle with swearing, lying, gossiping or being mean. Whatever sin or shortcoming it may be, you and I must always remember that our Lord Jesus Christ loves us. He loved us to the point of incarnating into Man in order to take our place for death row. It was only through His holy crucifixion that we could be given redemption. Even the passage of the 9th hour prayer states, "You who tasted death by the flesh at the third hour..." is one of the many examples of Christ's huge love for us to be with Him. So, logically speaking, why do we think after His tremendous sacrifice over 2000 years ago has expired in this day and age? Why are we choosing to foolishly think that He would not accept our true repentance now? You and I are the prodigal son (or maybe the older one at times—only God knows); but cut to the chase, as the Father accepted the Prodigal Son's repentance with open arms, the same will always happen to YOU.

Sayings of the Fathers

A certain monk told me that when he was very sick, his mother said to his father, "How our little boy is suffering. I would gladly give myself to be cut up into pieces if that would ease his suffering." Such is the love of God for people. He pitied people so much, that, he wanted to suffer for them, like their own mother and even more. But no one can understand this great love without the grace of the Holy Spirit (St. Silouan the Athonite, IX.10, Wisdom from Mount Athos: The Writings of Staretz Silouan, 1866 – 1938).

"I beg and beseech you, Lord, grant to all who have gone astray a true knowledge of you, so that each and every one may come to know your glory" (St. Isaac the Syrian).

People Places and Things

Saint Paul who was originally called Saul and practiced Judaism, was chosen by God to have a relationship with Him and to preach so that others may be lovers of Christ. An impressive total of thirteen books, in the New Testament, are known for certain to be written by Saint Paul. In Ephesians 1:7-10, Saint Paul highlights that since the time of creation, God already had you and I in His mind. Jesus Christ came into the world for bringing us closer to Him. He came to claim back what was His—you and I. This passage from Saint Paul is one of the gems in our faith because it illustrates everything that our Lord Jesus Christ came to do—to restore us and the world into our original blameless state.

Four Fantastic Facts

1. Saint Paul was born in 4 A.D. and died by martyrdom (condemned by Emperor Nero) on 64 A.D. in Italy.
2. Saint Paul changed the course of Christianity as an Apostle, theologian and letter-writer.
3. Saint Paul was one of the very few apostles who believed that the Gentiles were deserving to become Christians without circumcision. He even brought this idea to the leaders in Jerusalem; the Jerusalem council agreed with Saint Paul and changed the laws. so that. the

Gentiles could convert to Christianity without becoming circumcised (Jews) first.

4. Saint Paul was an advocate for gender equality. Being one of the greatest Early Church founders, He gave women opportunities for leadership in the ministries at Rome e.g. Phoebe, Aquila and Priscilla, Andronicus and Juniar.

Liturgical

In the consecration prayers from the Liturgy according to St. Cyril, we remember our Lord's incarnation and show our eternal gratitude by reciting:

"Amen, Amen, Amen. Your death, O Lord, we proclaim. Your Holy resurrection and ascension, we confess. We praise You; we bless You; we thank You, O Lord, and we entreat You, O our God."

As we grow older, it gets easier to reach a plateau in such liturgical responses like these. After all, we hear and recite it in every Divine Liturgy, at the same time and same place more or less. So what is the new revelation that we could possibly encounter? Sometimes we may even foolishly think that God is somewhat patriotic and in need of our constant affirmation. But truth be told, nothing could be further from the truth. It is vital for us to take the scripture in the Divine Liturgy in context. The Holy Spirit that resides in each one of us, will give us fresh insight and application as we attend and recite these liturgical responses.

Reflection

The Word became flesh to make us 'partakers of the divine nature'. For this is why, the Word became man and the Son of God became the Son of man; so that man, by entering into communion with the Word and thus receiving divine adoption, might become a son of God (Saint Athanasius).

God came from His Glory and Honour in Heaven above to bear our sin through the cross. If that was not humble enough, He carried our thoughts, actions and attitudes on His shoulders while on the cross. Some of these sins were mine and some were yours. Hitherto, our God had no regret incarnating as Man to receive us through a Divine adoption.

This Divine adoption shows that God did not die for an institution but individuals. God did not die for us to just pray in a church; He died for us to be the church and bring everyone—the broken, down-trodden, lost and bruised, to Him.

Chapter Two

Divine Intervention

As covered in the previous chapter, in consequence of death and corruption entering the world, the human race was in a perpetual process of destruction. It was only until God incarnated into Man and died on the cross; that mankind and all His creation could be saved. Many times one can ponder on why God, being above all, couldn't just go back on His word—especially when the devil's deceit had damned mankind to begin with. In saying that, it was just as unfitting for God to see His creation perish; God being a God of love, justice and truth, found it unworthy to contradict His word.

What a dilemma! From a human perspective, it would have been better for God to have not created mankind to begin with! And if it was unthinkable for God to go back on His word, then He should have been at ease to just let humankind perish in corruption—that they inflicted upon themselves. Sounds harsh right? It's humorous that sometimes we have that attitude towards our brothers, sisters and even ourselves. Whenever the Holy Spirit may nudge us for a particular mission, we choose to be corrupted by comfort. Thoughts play in our mind to justify our reason to live a comfortable life.

Not even repentance could be enough to mark humankind as incorruptible again. The remission of sins required bloodshed. The only perfect sacrifice that could compensate for all mankind, was our Lord Jesus Christ. At this assertion, His Divine intervention came. Moved with compassion and pity, He willed to die in our place. So, He stooped down to our level by incarnating as Man through the Holy Spirit and Virgin Mary. Out of His love, He—the Artificer revealed himself in human flesh—remaining pure and untainted by anyone. The corruption could not disappear without the price of death. And God chose to assume not a true human body that would encounter a human death.

By God's Divine intervention, the law of death upon us all was exterminated. As well as, we the corruptible, gained a fresh start and hope of a Joyous Resurrection.

Show Me a Sign!

Show me a sign! An exclamatory sentence we verbally or internally utter more than we like to admit. Even though God has shown His Divine intervention in our lives each day, we unfortunately do not measure it. Speaking from the chief culprit, we get spiritual amnesia when a prayer or two is not answered or answered the way we want. We forget all the good blessings God has showered us with and all the times He has helped us; we cry out, "Show me a sign." Why is that? Why is it when some of our prayers make us wait for an answer or God makes it clear that the answer is NO; that we decline in our faith, trust and love for Him? Let's not be like the Israelites, who, journeyed for 40 years to reach the Promised Land instead of 11 days because of their grumbling. Their grumbling and complaining blinded them to seeing God's Divine intervention in their lives. Likewise, when we do this, we become blind to both God's plan for us and we belittle His Divine intervention that happened over 2000 years ago—His incarnation to set us incorruptible and free again.

Sayings of the Fathers

"The truly intelligent man pursues one sole objective: to obey and to conform to the God of all... For it is absurd to be grateful to doctors who give us bitter and unpleasant medicines to cure our bodies, and yet to be ungrateful to God for what appears to us to be harsh, not grasping that all we encounter is for our benefit and in accordance with His providence. For knowledge of God and faith in Him is the salvation and perfection of the soul" (Saint Anthony the Great).

"The Son of God came to earth and became man, that, He might lead man into heaven and make him once again a citizen of Paradise; returning to him his original state of sinlessness and wholeness and uniting him unto Himself. By the action of Divine grace grated through the Church, a man's effort is also required. God saves His fallen creature by His own love for him. However, man's love for his Creator is also necessary; without it he cannot by saved. Striving towards God and cleaving unto the Lord by its humble love, the human soul obtains power to cleanse itself from sin and to strengthen itself for the struggle to complete victory over sin" (St. John the Wonderworker of Shanghai and San Francisco).

People Places and Things

Saint John the Wonderworker was an intensely active Arch Bishop of Shanghai and San Francisco. This Saint was exceedingly humble and would avoid any glory from people on his services and prayers. Saint John the Wonderworker completed many miracles during his lifetime and was renowned for directing everyone to glorify and boast in God's divine intervention alone.

Four Fantastic Facts

1. Saint John the Wonderworker was born on the 4th of June, 1896 and died on the 2nd of July 1966.
2. Saint John the Wonderworker's baptismal name was Michael—after Archangel Michael.
3. Saint John the Wonderworker was consecrated bishop on May 28, 1934 over the diocese of Shanghai.
4. In 1962, Abp. John was assigned to the Diocese of San Francisco, succeeding his long-time friend Arch Bishop Tikhon. He was able to bring peace and unity within the congregation of the new cathedral there.

Liturgical

From the prayers of reconciliation in Saint Gregory's Liturgy, the priest narrates our God's Divine intervention through the following testimonial: "For You are the one who is able to lift all sin and remove the injustices and the lawlessness of wretched men. You are the purity of the whole world."

This depiction by Saint Gregory, beautifully captures the essence of God's divine intervention for us. It also strengthens us to regard how much God has done for us in the past, whenever our faith and trust in Him is dwindled.

Reflection

Is our faith strengthened to see God's Divine intervention? From the basic necessities to the opportunities and dreams coming true, do we take it as a matter of chance or a part of God's purpose? Living in this 21st century, it is too common to consider successes as our own. To add, in the competitive workforce, employees are even encouraged to being proud and arrogant to gain power over others. Undoubtedly, being Christians, this attitude and norm, makes it more challenging to maintain humility. I emphasise with the word—challenging. It is not impossible for us to remember who we were before—damned creations in need of a Divine intervention. Remember, God was humble to the point of considering us as precious to sacrifice for. May we join King David in wholeheartedly praying: "What is man that You are mindful of him, or the son of man that You care for him?" Also, may we follow God's Divine intervention as a timeless model for us on how to live—selflessly, lovingly and sacrificial.

Chapter Three

When There Is a Will, God Makes the Way

God, the Artificer, the Incorporeal and Uncreated took pity on the limitation of mankind. Therefore, He did not leave them destitute of the knowledge of Himself or their very existence. Through God's grace, it was sufficient for Him to safeguard them from their own neglect, defilement and lusts. Even when our ancestors invented various gods to worship, God forgave their neglect of His grace. Likewise, when we as Saint Paul puts it, "Worship the creature, rather than the Creator," such as our work, our beauty, our studies, talents, electronic devices or our pride, God also is open to forgive our lost respect for Him. Our God is a God for harmony. His love and goodness saves us from the moments of fraud and illusion and lift us towards the truth.

When a portrait panel becomes destroyed with external stains, the artist does not throw the subject of the portrait but re-draws it on another panel. Just the same, God being the artist of mankind, deemed it unfitting to leave us stained in our sin, so He re-painted us into His ineffable image and likeness again.

Not only is God an artist, but a good teacher. Like a good teacher reaches her pupils level to influence them with the content, our God reached our level of simplicity to influence us to attain the wisdom of God.

God, the Saviour of us all and the Word, out of His great love, chose to subject Himself to manifest into the body and senses of a human in order to meet us half-way. He was born to die and rise in order to recall you and I from the path of destruction. Forwarding this point in God's own words, He says, "I came to seek and to save that which was lost" (Luke 19:10).

We, as merely humans, are limited. It is not possible for us to transport from one place to another with our minds. For God on the other hand, moving the sun and stars by just a command is possible. God is limitless and His works are imperceptible for a limited human. God was not hedged in by His human body as people may think. The body was not a limitation to His Divinity but an instrument. While on our Earth, He did not cease being the King of Kings and ruler of the entire universe and creation. While He moved to and fro on the Earth, He at the same time moved the entire universe by His mind and invisible might. Even at the point of the cross, He, the Son, was in a constant union with the Divine Father. He shared our human nature in everything but sin alone. He proved Himself to be the son of God through extraordinary acts such as healing diseases, driving away evil spirits and confronted the unbelieving Jews by underlining: "If I do not the works of My Father, believe Me not; but if I do, even if ye believe not Me, believe My works, that ye may know that the Father is in Me and I in the Father" (John 10:38). Here, our God is proclaiming that, His Godhead is veiled in human nature; His bodily feelings of hunger, thirst, hurt and joy prove that, He is a man, but His wondrous works also prove that His Divinity never departed from His humanity.

You Are Always on God's Mind

"How precious are Your thoughts to me, O God! How great is the sum of them! If I should count them, they would be more in number than the sand; When I awake, I am still with You" (Psalm 139: 17, 18).

This Psalm illustrates three things about God: (1) His thoughts being different to ours, (2) His ways being higher than ours and (3) His care being sufficient.

God remembers our frailty. He not only formed us as humans but also incarnated into one. He understands when we feel betrayed or denied in the world, as He was betrayed from Judas and denied by Peter. God understands when we feel alone or rejected, as He was left to be judged by Pontius Pilate alone and be rejected by His own people. Those times when we sin or reach a point where we just feel condemned, God wants us to know, that, He has us on His mind all the time. He never wants us to feel hopeless—especially when He promises as written in the Psalm above, that, He never forgets us. Just as a father, mother or sibling is protective over their loved ones and it breaks their heart to see them hurt, it pains God all the more to see us in a pitiful state. What is changed? God's love from the beginning of time was strong enough to save the pitiful state of mankind's damnation and restore them up to become children of God once again. Now in this time and age, our God's great love remains for us and the world. God being real, eternal and not a figment of imagination, exceeds the fictional superheroes in our world; There is hope! So whenever you find yourself in that dark pit, keep your striking smile on because God has YOU on His mind and sees YOU. When there is a will, God will make a way. Nothing worth coming ever comes easy. Just take a deep breath, pause and when you pause, reflect on how to be patient and pray.

Sayings of the Fathers

Remember, never to fear the power of evil more than your trust in the power and love of God (Hermas, one of the Seventy).

"God, who is by nature good and dispassionate, loves all men equally as His handiwork. But He glorifies the virtuous man because in his will he is united to God. At the same time, in His goodness he is merciful to the sinner and by chastising him in this life brings him back to the path of virtue. Similarly, a man of good and dispassionate judgment also loves all men equally. He loves the virtuous man because of his nature and the probity of his intention; and he loves the sinner, too, because of his nature and because in his compassion he pities him for foolishly stumbling in darkness" (St. Maximos the Confessor).

People Places and Things

Tyler Doherty was born on the 23rd of September, the year 1995. This boy was brought up in Nashville Tennessee, USA; he loved to play soccer and was a very spiritual boy. On top of prayer, Tyler would talk to God through letters. God for Tyler was not far away. In spite of his rare condition of brain cancer, Tyler remained positive that God's will had a purpose in His life. This little boy's strength and positivity helped his family remain strong in their faith and hope. Like a flower that is plucked out when it has blossomed, Tyler—a warrior of God, passed away from his brain cancer on the 7th of March, 2005. He was only nine years old at the time. Now, over a decade later, his legacy for people to write letters to God as in his words 'God has each of us in His mind' lives on.

Four Fantastic Facts

1. A total of 30 radiation treatments over the course of four months could not stop the cancer from taking over Tyler's brain.

2. During Tyler's hospital treatments, his father was inspired by him and began writing letters to God in his journal.

3. Tyler's story led to his father writing a movie script on Tyler's life and legacy. This movie is called 'Letters to God'.

4. Tyler wrote letters to God and actually sent them to the mailboxes in his neighbourhood. The postal carrier would read Tyler's letters and was touched by them so much that he became Christian himself.

Liturgical

In the prayer of confession from Saint Gregory's liturgy, the priest confesses our faith claiming, "Amen. Amen. Amen.

I believe, I believe, I believe and profess to the last breath, that this is the life-giving Body that You took. O Christ my God, from the lady of us all, 139, the holy Theotokos Saint Mary, You made It One with Your divinity without mingling, without confusion and without alteration."

The priest recites this on behalf of us all. Our faith, I daresay, would be worthless if we did not believe this foundation in our faith; that God's divinity and humanity were intertwined when He was on this Earth. I echo Saint Paul who affirms me and says, "If Christ (as a man) has not been raised (through divinity of God), our preaching is worthless, and so is our faith" (1 Corinthians 15:14).

Reflection

God is not a God of confusion, but peace. Observe your emotions and feelings right now. What do you feel? No matter what predicament or difficulty you are facing, the Lord has a way for enabling His sovereign power working in our life. In fact, God majors in showing His power in hopeless situations. Take for instance, Israel. When the Israelites were in a place that they could not cross, God parted the red sea into two before them (Exodus 13: 17-14:32). Or take Daniel's example, who when spitefully sent to the lion's den, was protected from any harm (Daniel 6: 10-23). The Word is in every dimension above; you and I need to increase in being Christ like in our thoughts, deeds and words when in adverse circumstances. Never forget that whenever you have reached a 'dead end', submit yourself to the God—when there is our will, He will always make a Way.

Chapter Four

Mightier Than Death

To recap, Christ is revealed as God and Son of God. He is the Word who orders all things and sent His only begotten Son to teach and save mankind from the sting of death and the worship of idols. But, above all that, there was a debt for our sin from the Fall of Adam and Eve that had to be paid by the shedding of blood. That is the reason, that, the Word willed to dwell among us. Namely, He came on this Earth so that He might be the perfect sacrifice and free mankind from the account of primal transgression.

In spite of His body being uniquely formed from Virgin Mary and the Holy Spirit, his body was liable to death. The death of all mankind was consummated in the Lord's body. The Saviour of the world died on our behalf, so that, we who believe in Him, would no longer die but be promised immortality. This triumph is divinely expressed by Saint Paul who writes:

"Death is swallowed up in victory. O Death, where is your sting? O Grave, where is your victory?" (1 Corinthians 15: 55)

Our God surrendered Himself in the place of us all in public. The public display of His crucifixion shows strength, not weakness. Our Lord chose to not die a quiet death as it would be like any man's death—hindering the glory of His Resurrection. That is why He chose an extremely gory death to die as a ransom for all and rise after three days in perfect soundness.

To reiterate, the ultimate reason for His coming was to be the monument of mankind's victory over death. Truly, the Jews' plot showed no limitation or weakness to our Lord. That is why, we feel bittersweet to them especially as their plot to kill our Lord was exactly what our Lord pursued—He waited for death to assure mankind of the future Resurrection. His death had to precede resurrection, for there could be no resurrection without it. The disciples of our Lord were even afraid, in spite of the Lord constantly telling them, that, He would rise again after three days. So imagine if our Lord died a secret and unwitnessed death—instead of a public one. This would have left the disciples even more confused and with absolutely no proof to support His Glorious Resurrection. Accordingly, the disciples would also have no boldness to even speak about the Lord's Resurrection, if they did not witness that He had first died.

As a wrestler does not choose his antagonists, our Lord allowed His spectators to choose whatever death sentence they wanted in order for Him to vindicate His superior strength. The cross was expedient for Him to bear the curse that was on all of mankind. Our Lord came to overthrow the devil and purify us to be heirs again to Heaven. He cleansed the air through his death on the cross and re-opened the gates of Heaven and made our path to salvation possible again.

He Is Our Guide Unto Death

"Lift up your heads, O gates. Be lifted up, O ancient doors, that the King of Glory may enter" (Psalm 24: 7).

Our Lord Jesus Christ is the gate. Through His death, all mankind could enter into the gate leading to the glory of God's eternal presence. To think of the promise of immortality with our God should not be seen as scary or dark. God wants us to live our lives as what it is—a gift. He has perfectly ordained each of our life chapters to give us joy, peace and love. Christianity is not meant to be seen as just a struggle or a faith based on solely tribulations. Christianity is having joy, peace and love in the midst of the good and the tribulations. Our God desires us to be joyful with Him on this Earth and ever after. Even when we go through griefs, heartbreak and troubles, He will gently remind us of His promises. It takes two in this relationship; God plays His part, but we must play ours too.

We play our part by pleading through prayer—communication, having union with Him through Holy Communion and choosing to come out into the light again. Let us praise and sing, "This God is our God for ever and ever; he will be our Guide even unto death." Our God is good and He will always touch us, will love and grace in every condition, pressure, insecurity and obstacle we face.

Sayings of the Fathers

The Most-High planted in the middle of Paradise, the thrice blessed wood, the gift of life for us, in approaching it, Adam might find eternal and immortal life; he did not strive earnestly to know this life; he failed to attain it, and revealed death. However, the robber, seeing how the plant in Eden had been beautifully transplanted in Golgotha, recognized the life in it and said to himself, "This is what my father lost formerly In Paradise" (St. Romanos the Melodist).

"Let us glorify God! With the coming of the Son of God in the flesh upon the earth, with His offering Himself up as a sacrifice for the sinful human race, there is given to those who believe the blessing of the Heavenly Father, replacing that curse which had been uttered by God in the beginning; they are adopted and receive the promise of an eternal inheritance of life. To a humanity orphaned by reason of sin, the Heavenly Father returns anew through the mystery of re-birth, that is, through baptism and repentance. People are freed of the torment-ing, death-bearing authority of the devil, of the afflictions of sin and of various passions" (St. John of Kronstadt).

People Places and Things

Outside the gates of Jerusalem, Golgotha was the place where our Lord Jesus Christ was sentenced to be crucified in. For the Romans at the time, this spot was a place kept for cap-ital punishment and would warn travellers of the city that criminality was not tolerated. The sovereignty of God fulfilled the scriptures from Genesis 3: 15, that states, "It shall bruise thy head and thou shalt bruise his heel." Our Lord crushed the skull of Satan as prophesied and that is why Golgotha perfectly symbolized that—this connection was not a coincidence. In this twenty-first century, tourists including you and I can visit Golgotha by booking in a Christian group tour in Jerusalem; this tour is called the 'Skull Hill tour'.

Four Fantastic Facts

1. The Holy Bible teaches us, that, after David slew Goliath, he cut off his head and brought the skull to Jerusalem. Many scholars theorise that Golgotha received its' name from Goli-ath's head being buried there.

2. Golgotha, when observed closely, has rocks

resembling two eye sockets, a nose and on a whole, it looks like a skull.

3. Along with Christ's tomb, Golgotha is located within the walled Old city of Jerusalem at the Church of the Holy Sepulchre.
4. Golgotha is considered as the pre-eminent shrine for Christians and one of the holiest places on Earth. According to credible sources, a thousand of people on average, pay homage at Golgotha every day.

Liturgical

In the prayer of Consecration from St. Cyril's Divine Liturgy, the priest prays, "For every time you shall eat of this bread and drink of this cup, you proclaim My death, confess My resurrection and remember Me till come." This represents our Christ reminding you and I on His death, and how through His death, we have gained fellowship with Him and forgiveness of our sins. Not only that, our Lord Jesus Christ calls us to remember how He was betrayed, how He willed to be broken and shed His blood so that our souls may live. The fullness of His love and power is food to our soul indeed. This spiritual feast we encounter in Holy Communion nourishes our hearts and reminds us on our blessings. To count our blessings is a great habit to reach satisfaction and defeat the power of sin in our everyday lives.

Reflection

The greatest love story that will remain until the end of time, is, the crucifixion of our Lord Jesus Christ. Jesus's self sacrifice and suffering for humanity merits our value. When we look at ourselves and put ourselves down in the mask of humility, this displeases God. To be humble is to think of yourself as valued by a God and used by God for His divine purpose. God loved you and I to death. His death transformed us to no longer be defined by our sins, but by God's love for us. God's loving kindness exists from the rising of the sun to its setting. Our weaknesses, our shortcomings and pitiful states do not move God away from us. God died for us to repent and He will always accept our sincere repentance. Remember that He loved us too much to leave us in a sinful state. The finest way we can show our appreciation for His love for us, is to, mirror His love in this world. By mirroring God's love in our everyday lives, we can subject this world of hatred, lies, envy and pride to convert into a world of love, truth and joy all the time.

Chapter Five

The Victorious Resurrection

Our Lord, Jesus Christ, made all creation witness His death on the cross in order to erase any doubt that His sacred, impassable and incorruptible body, would rise from the third day. The short interval of three days between his death and His victorious Resurrection, was a token of glory through the trampling of death once and for all.

The disciples and righteous people who mourned and were even afraid from our Lord Jesus Christ's death, were the same ones who witnessed His Resurrection. For them to witness and embrace the Resurrection, they received living proof on Christ's new promise for mankind's immortality. All the prior doubts about Christ's conquest over death were diminished. To the extent, that, the disciples and believers became witnesses of His marvellous Resurrection—some even to the point of martyrdom.

Before our Lord Jesus Christ's death, death used to be strong and terrible, but since Christ's mounting on the cross, death was trampled under Christ Himself. When we do the sign of the cross, we receive power, love and grace that cannot be robbed from us anymore.

When a snake is trampled, regardless of its specimen, no one doubts that it is dead and bereft of any strength. Our Lord Jesus Christ is the same. He completely died and then rose after three days to make death completely powerless to you and I—believers and bearers of the sign of the cross. By His death, he destroyed death and by His Resurrection, He gave us life with God. Saint Paul eloquently writes this point as: "The death He died, He died to sin once for all; but the life He lives, He lives to God" (Romans 6:10).

God had humanity but is not limited to a human level— after all His divinity was still intact. No evil spirit in the Earth could even endure His Name or presence. Take the instance of the evil spirits who cried out, "And he (evil spirits) shouted in a loud voice, "What do You want with me, Jesus, Son of the Most-High God? I beg You before God not to torture me"" (Mark 5:7). If the evil spirits could know that God was the Father manifest, it is silly for us to doubt the power and wisdom of God descending, dying and resurrecting for ultimately us.

Think of the blind men and women on this Earth that we may encounter. Despite not being able to see the sun, they do not doubt that the sun is there because they feel the warmth, heat and light. Similarly, even when we may be blinded in our faith due to her lax attitude and sins, we can be brought to our faith again and resurrect through God's warmth—a warmth that loves, comforts and re-routes us back on our paths to salvation whenever we go astray.

From the confession of the evil spirits or God's individual impact in our lives, you and I can be daily witnesses that God undoubtedly raised His own body over 2000 years ago, to destroy death. The destruction of death raised us to join Him in a victory over death and attain the promise of immortality and incorruption.

We Are Victorious

The death of our Lord Jesus Christ is victorious for us only if we trust in God. Families and friendships can only grow when trust is a foundation. To trust someone is to love them. To trust God is to love God. One cannot say they love God but not trust Him. For whenever something may not go to plan, those who do not trust God, will not see or wait on His divine purpose—leading them to be separated from His love. The victory of His Resurrection makes us confident that we will have a victory over death too. Now thinking about this in the present, when we chose to believe in God's Word, we will not be scared when we lose a loved one.

I emphasize on the word—scared. It will and can hurt to lose a loved one and it is perfectly normal to express it—Jesus Himself cried when He lost Lazarus. Cut to the chase, the difference of perceiving death through Christian lenses, is that, we have an eternal hope in death. Death is not the end after all. Rather, death is a second life where we live a new life of righteousness and victory due to our prior repentance and live forever in His love.

Sayings of the Fathers

"The gateway to divine repentance has been opened; let us enter eagerly, purified in our bodies and observing abstinence from food and passions, as obedient servants of Christ who has called the world into the heavenly Kingdom. Let us offer to the King of all a tenth part of the whole year, that we may look with love upon His Resurrection" (Sessional hymn, Matins, Cheesefare Monday).

"And the Word became flesh! In order to make us earthly beings into heavenly ones; in order to make sinners into saints; in order to raise us up from corruption into incorruption, from earth to heaven; from enslavement to sin and the devil—into the glorious freedom of children of God; from death—into immortality, in order to make us sons of God and to seat us together with Him upon the Throne as His royal children. O, boundless compassion of God! O, inexpressible wisdom of God! O, great wonder, astounding not only the human mind, but the angelic (mind) as well!" (St. John of Kronstadt)

People Places and Things

Joan of Arc was a peasant girl who lived in Medieval France. Archangel Michael was sent by God to ascribe her to lead the French army and give it victory over its long war with England. After Joan of Arc convinced Prince Charles of Valois, she was given the role as the commander of the army and guided the French army to achieve this momentous victory. Alas, in 1431, at the age of 19, Joan of Arc was burnt at the stake for the numerous accusations that she was not holy, but a witch. Joan of Arc faced her death sentence with such courage as the martyrs and modern-day martyrs that our Church cherishes. Joan of Arc's endurance, proves that, she held onto the promise of her victory over death and the Lord's place for her in Heaven above.

Four Fantastic Facts

Joan of Arc was allowed to be the commander of the French army but was forbidden to participate in active combat.

Joan of Arc's bob haircut inspired France from 1909. Many people in Joan of Arc's memory, would deliberately request their hairdressers to give them a bob haircut.

Joan of Arc was falsely accused for sorcery. Despite her false accusations (A total of 70), she followed in our Lord Jesus Christ's footsteps and kept silent until she was burnt at the stake.

Pope Benedict XV canonized her as a Saint in 1920. This inspired France to make Joan of Arc their patron saint.

Reflection

Death is depicted by the Holy Bible as the mortal enemy. However, being Christians, we have no fear for this enemy because we believe in the wonderful secret God has revealed to us—the victory of the Resurrection. To believe in the victory of the Resurrection is more than celebrating our Lord's stunning Resurrection; it is to celebrate that none of us will die but be transformed. Our hope from our Lord Jesus Christ's Resurrection is knowing that one day, we will be in the presence of the Father and Son for all eternity.

For now, we can live for Him and reflect on the 'resurrection moments' that we have experienced in this life so far. Perhaps, it was defeating a sin, seeing God through an illness, loss, accident or failure. Whatever it may be my friend, expect many more of those mini Resurrections to come.

Keep strong, keep steady in His love and rejoice in your promise of a Resurrection!

Chapter Six

Rejected By His Own

The Jews and Gentiles who missed out in accepting Christ as their Saviour respectively, ridiculed their disbelief in the Lord Jesus Christ to the point of sentencing Him to death, in spite of the scriptures foretelling on the marvel of the Messiah's birth from a Virgin and Holy Spirit (Isaiah 7:14); to His death and glorious Resurrection to follow (Psalm 16:10; Isaiah 53:11), the stubborn Jews and Gentiles refused to believe.

On the contrary, the Jews and Gentiles deliberately ignored the Scriptures and prophecies that they read and lawlessly plotted to make Jesus suffer by their own hands. The Creator was rejected by His own creation. He chose to be dishonoured to bear our sins. He chose to be afflicted to make us healed. He chose to be treated lawlessly to spring back our dignity. Due to our sins, He was brought to death for our sake. The prophecies on the manner of His death as foretold by Moses (Deuteronomy 28:26) and Isaiah (Isaiah 53:5), were fulfilled.

These are just two examples of the various prophetic proofs that our Lord Jesus Christ was the Messiah and that the unbelieving Jews and Gentiles were the instigators for the prophecies to take place.

These unbelievers tried to justify, that, our Lord could not be a great man or the King of Kings. They investigated the prophets from the lineage of Abraham to Jesse and concluded their case of making an enmity with our Lord on every side. The investigations were not true and the scriptures were taken out of context to suggest that our Lord was not the Messiah, but a man like Isaiah, Jeremiah or Ezekiel who suffered not for the sake of all.

In spite of all the evidence from the miracles our Lord did, such as, healing the blind, lame, maimed and raising the dead, the Jews and Gentiles were not moved to stop indulging in their narrative—that the Messiah was yet to come. Their deliberate and shameless denial of the facts, proves that, they were irreligious heathens and hypocrites as our Lord Jesus Christ coined.

Now I must emphasize, that, the Lord remained patient and tried again and again to wake them up to believe and not be so blind. However, in love, our Lord gave us all free will. So, it remained up to them to choose to believe in Him or simply to not. Unsurprisingly, these unbelieving Jews and Gentiles chose to remain like an unreasonable person, who, sees that the Earth is clearly lit up by the sun but denies the sun existing.

What a shame! The whole world became enlightened with the Divine teaching about His sacrifice and legacy. Leaving the unbelieving Jews and Gentiles taking a subconscious atheism resulted to the most appalling consequence— separation from God.

Be Humble, Not a Hypocrite

Too often, we can humour on how blind and hypocritical the unbelieving Jews and Gentiles were; forgetting the times that we can deviate from Jesus in diverse ways. We should not get comfortable and feel 'safe', that, we do not fall into the category of 'hypocrite'. Instead, we should benefit from the unbelieving Jews and Gentiles fate and ponder on what sins or shortcomings separate us from God. To practice such serious reflection on our progress should not be depressing. Just as humility helps us keep record of our grades and comments in order to learn what and how to improve or maintain high results, we must be humble to keep record of our spiritual progress. Also, just as we invest our time, emotions and properties in our relationships, the same investment with God has to occur—especially if you want it to flourish. I close with this reminder, as we recite in the concluding prayer in the Agpeya, that, "Our God has a great desire to save everyone from sin and death and judgment." Remember, that, this desire includes YOU. So, choose humility and find yourself never separated from God, as you will always grip onto the need of His salvation.

Sayings of the Fathers

"If you would be simple-hearted like the Apostles, would not conceal your human short-comings, would not pretend to be especially pious, if you would walk free from hypocrisy, then that is the path. While it is easy, not every-one can find it or understand it. This path is the shortest way to salvation and attracts the grace of God. Unpretentiousness, guilelessness, frankness of soul—this is what is pleasing to the Lord, Who is lowly of heart. Except ye become like children, ye shall not enter into the Kingdom of God (Matt. 18:13)" (Elder Leonid of Optina).

"Let all involuntary suffering teach you to remember God, and you will not lack occasion for repentance" (St. Mark the Ascetic).

People Places and Things

Saint Marcelino was a boy found in front of a Franciscan Monastery at Spain, abandoned by his mother when he was just a baby. The monks looked after him as their own. According to the friars of the monastery, Saint Marcelino was a bright, curious and cheeky boy. Regardless, the friars of the monastery deeply loved him. When Saint Marcelino was only five years old, he played soccer in the monastery attic. One day of his daily plays of soccer, he accidently hit a life sized statue of the Crucified Lord. When he went to apologize, the Lord Jesus Christ appeared to him as the Crucified Lord. Saint Marcelino gave Him food and water every day from that divine appearance. Saint Marcelino would talk every day with the Lord on several topics—especially about missing his mother. The monks heard every now and then, Marcelino talking in the attic, but they assumed that he was simply talking to himself. The one day that the friars decided to check up on Marcelino in the attic, they witnessed Marcelino conversing with the Crucified Lord and taken by Him to be reunited with his dead mother. After this magnificent occurrence, the friars in the monastery buried the crucified Lord in the Chapel and buried Marcelino situated next to it.

Four Fantastic Facts

1. One of the cheekiest acts Marcelino did, was, releasing animals to be free during a Spanish festival. Although Saint Marcelino's intentions were purely to stop the animals from being abused, this caused havoc in the town.

2. At first, Saint Marcelino did not know that the Crucified Christ was talking to Him. It was only until the Crucified Christ gave Him his

first Holy Communion, that, He realised He was the Christ.

3. The monks witnessed the miracle through a crack in the attic door and burst in just in time, to see the dead Marcelino bathed in a heavenly glow.

4. Saint Marcelino's body currently remains to be buried underneath the chapel in Spain and is venerated by many who visit the monastery.

Reflection

Our Lord Jesus Christ desires to be believed as our salvation, but then again, He also yearns for us to see Him as our best friend and confidant. God has given us all from our Baptism, His Holy Spirit to counsel, to teach and to comfort us personally. Our God is a great God and is zealous for each one of us to be grounded in His word and accept His advice and presence—as we would of a friend. I encourage you to join me and diminish anything that mediates our relationship with God. Everything we say and do from the spheres of the church, our family, work, school and social life, should point us to Him—the fullness of our joy.

Chapter Seven

The Power of Love

Now, this is proof that, although this world is temporal and will pass away, Christ, being God the Word, will always remain. The prophets and teachers contributions have been inspired from God to teach us on the manifestation of our God to save us indeed. Instead of fearing death, the saints and martyrs who read from these divine scriptures, longed to suffer for Him as they held onto the promise of their Resurrection and incorruptibility.

In our Lord's second coming as described in the book of Revelations, He will come not in lowliness, but ineffable glory. He will not subject Himself to the humiliation from the unbelieving Jews and Gentiles, but bestow Himself on us with His proper majesty and glory. Unlike his unjust death judgement by Pontius Pilate, He will be the judge for each one of us and judge us according to our deeds. For the good and believing, they will hear the joyful voice from the Sovereign saying, "Well done, good and faithful servant; you were faithful over a few things,

I will make you ruler over many things. Enter into the joy of your Lord" (Matthew 25:21). On the other hand, those who willingly practiced evil are sentenced for eternal darkness and fire. It is up to us to prepare ourselves for that terrific day. The Scriptures, many times, remind us to prepare and watch for the splendid coming of the Son of Man, upon the clouds of Heaven in the glory of the Father; it will happen at an hour we do not expect. Blessed Paul forwards this and writes, "For we must all appear before the judgment seat of Christ, that each one may receive the things done in the body, according to what he has done, whether good or bad" (1 Corinthians 5:10).

Following the saints example, we must keep searching for the right understanding of the Scriptures and value the Scriptures as the framework, that guides us to live a pure, good and virtuous life. Our human nature may be limited but it can be challenged. Our Lord Jesus Christ took our humanity and was able to remain pure in all His deeds. You may argue that, this is because, He had His Divinity intact with Him— and that is valid. However, as far as our human nature can cope, we similarly can be cleansed and reach an approximate level of His purity, by imitating the saints and martyrs. Remember, the saints and martyrs were humans just like us, but they approached their lives in such a sacred way, that, many things were revealed to them by God and they have the gift to intercede for us.

Without a doubt, we desire to be like the saints and martyrs and have our place laid up in the Kingdom of Heaven. To be capable of receiving this Heavenly ruling, we must first cleanse our lives, imitate the saints and martyrs deeds and unite ourselves in fellowship with life— God. By doing this, we will escape the peril of sinners and receive the promise that is written, rather, as it is written, "No eye has seen, no ear has heard, no heart has imagined, what God has prepared for those who love Him" (1 Corinthians 2:9).

What are you waiting for? Take the pledge to live a godly life and embrace the power of love.

Glory be to the Father in Christ Jesus and our Lord with the Son Himself in the Holy Spirit. May glory, honour and might be unto the age of ages. Amen.

Holy Collision

The incarnation of our Lord Jesus Christ, would have had no meaning without the Cross and His Holy Resurrection. This Cross was the place where God and sinful mankind embarked on a Holy Collision. The Holy Collision cost God His life, but He deemed it worth all the pain to open the gates of salvation to us again.

To be greedy in the passing things of this world is vanity, but to be greedy for Heaven is wisdom. Evaluate yourself and do not discount what the incarnate God has offered us—the length of eternal life. Let us hold onto gratitude for His magnitude of love bestowed on us, to, be blessed with the privilege of eternal live in the glory of Heaven. Now to describe Heaven is unfathomable. Only can our narrow understanding be assured that Heaven is worth endeavouring for and resembles the hymns that say, "Heaven is a wonderful place."

Sayings of the Fathers

"If we make every effort to avoid death of the body, still, more should it be our endeavour to avoid death of the soul. There is no obstacle for a man who wants to be saved, other than, negligence and laziness of soul" (St. Anthony the Great).

"Pay attention carefully. After the sin comes, the shame; courage follows repentance. Did you pay attention to what I said? Satan upsets the order; he gives the courage to sin and the shame to repentance" (St. John Chrysostom).

People Places and Things

For Saint Augustine, the presence and activity of God was so common, that, he had little reason to believe in God's existence. Nor could he believe that God came incarnated as

Man to save mankind. As a result of such queries, Saint Augustine became an atheist from the age of nine and rejected his mother's plea to be baptized. Nevertheless, his beloved mother—Saint Monica, cried and prayed for a consecutive twenty years, just for him to believe in God. Saint Monica was thankful to God for Saint Augustine, as, he was a brilliant and talented student from his prime age to his youth. However, none of that mattered as he had lacked the ultimate truth. Yet, in due time, God finally answered Saint Monica's prayers and when Saint Augustine reached the age of 29 and worked as a successful teacher, Bishop Ambrose influenced him to give up his mundane centred life. Not only that, but Bishop Ambrose diminished Saint Augustine's doubt on the Godhead and the Holy Collision, impelling him to become baptized as a Christian.

Four Fantastic Facts

1. Saint Augustine, not only embraced Christianity from the age of 29, but he decided to live his life in celibacy and service to God.
2. By the grace of God, when Saint Augustine turned 38 years old, he was ordained as the wonderful Bishop of Hippo, Africa.
3. Saint Augustine was one of the greatest Christian writers of his time. His writing repertoire includes 113 books and treatises, 200+ letters

and 500+ sermons. Unfortunately, many of his writings are lost.

4. One of his iconic and lasting writings are called 'The Confessions'. Saint Augustine wrote the confessions when he was 75 years old.

Liturgical

In the prayers of the departed from St Cyril's Liturgy, we the congregation, recite the following to confirm our belief, that, grief, sorrow and groaning have fled away from His Holy Collision, "As it was, and shall be, from generation to generation. And unto the ages of all ages. Amen."

It is a comforting declaration and reminder to us all, that, our Lord's incarnation was given for our salvation, remission of sins and eternal life.

Reflection

We need to see, that, God incarnated as Man on Earth to not only die for us, but to live for us. What makes Him our everlasting Saviour, is dying for us all and at the same time, living a blameless life. Do not hesitate to come close to Him. Never let the devil make you think that you have to be at a 'level of goodness' before pursuing a relationship with God.

After all, if that was truly the case, there would have been no need for God to incarnate in the first place! He would have left all mankind to be erased perpetually and create new creations.

Truth be told, Jesus Christ took our sins on Himself willingly. His incarnation was meant for the purpose of covering us in His righteousness, gifting us with salvation and the choice to accept Him.

If a person such as an unbeliever, were to ask you to describe your relationship with God, what would you say?

I challenge you to read the following and reflect authentically on how certain you feel about these statements:

I feel peace from God that surpasses understanding (Romans 5:1).

I have confidence that God knows exactly what is best for me (John 5:14).

I am a beloved child of God (John 1:12).

I am an heir to eternal life with my Beloved Lord (John 5:24).

I am accepted by a God who forgives me always when I sincerely repent (Romans 3:22–23).

I am loved by God so much that I was deemed worthy to be atoned of my sins (1 John 4:9, 10).

My dear brothers and sisters in Christ, I plead you all to firmly cement in your minds, these statements of truth as foundations not for living a 'guilt-free' life, but to significantly keep growing in our spiritual understanding. Only by growing in our spiritual understanding of God, can we then actually love Him with all our heart, soul, mind and strength (Mark 12:28-30).